"FIRST CHORDS & HOW TO USE THEM"

By: WILBUR M. SAVIDGE

Photography . . . . .John McDearmon
Technical Supervision . . . . .Randy L. Vradenburg
Production Manager . . . . .W.M. Savidge
Proof Reading . . . . .Ken Nance
Typesetting .Team Graphix, Inc.
Printing . . . . .Vicks Lithograph & Printing Corp.

PRAXIS MUSIC PUBLICATIONS, INC.
HURST, TEXAS

A Word from the Author . . .

The guitar can be alot of fun! Everyone seems to be playing one, and surely it must be very easy to learn! It *is* fun, and many people are playing the instrument, but like most things in which we become involved, there is much more to playing the guitar than is at first apparent.

All too often, the first guitar is purchased without a factual understanding of the elements involved in playing correctly, and educational books all too often fail to provide critical information the beginner desperately requires. The first-time player is faced immediately with a decision: What do we mean when we proclaim — "Play Guitar"?

Generally we can, on the guitar, create music two ways: Strum chords, usually described as playing *Rhythm;* play notes, commonly referred to as playing the *Melody.* To play melodies, one must be able to sight-read, to look at a written note and determine its pitch and placement on the guitar fingerboard, or develop the ability to play·"by ear".

The knowledge of theory and the acquired musical skills to play written arrangements lie beyond most self-instruction. However, it is possible to learn to play chords without the help of a qualified teacher, provided the new student will take the time to learn a few fundamentals of music and how chords are played on the instrument.

I believe the material in this book, its sequence of presentation and special artwork will prove invaluable in your study of the guitar. I hope you find this book a valuable learning aid. Good luck!

— Bill Savidge

HOW TO USE THIS BOOK

This book covers:

- HOW TO PLAY THE GUITAR
- CHORDS BY KEY GROUPS
- CHORDS BY ALPHABETICAL NAME and
- HOW TO USE CHORDS.

Each page is a step-by-step, logical sequence of usable knowledge. You will be led through each phase of how to play, what chords are and how they are properly used. Chord diagrams (which resemble the guitar neck) will show you proper finger positions.

Each pair of pages covers a single idea, and is complete in itself. No terminology will appear that has not been already explained on preceding pages.

Unlike other basic chord books, we present (by diagrams and photographs) chords by key groups. This is the only way chords are used!

Rhythm patterns are explained and examples provided to teach you how to use chords and create rhythmic patterns to fit individual songs.

WHAT YOU MUST DO TO PLAY THE GUITAR

The guitar is fun, easy to play and offers a new challenge every time you pick it up. Being told what to do will not make you a good guitarist. These four things you must do:

- OWN A REASONABLY GOOD INSTRUMENT
- HAVE THE DESIRE TO LEARN TO PLAY
- OBTAIN THE KNOWLEDGE NECESSARY TO PLAY
- PRACTICE, PRACTICE, PRACTICE!

Remember, you MUST have the desire to play. You MUST know what to do, and you MUST practice. Without applying these concepts, you will never learn to play the guitar.

KNOW YOUR GUITAR

To play the guitar, we must first find out what the guitar is and how it works. Study the pictures and become an expert on the various parts of the guitar.

THE HEADSTOCK. The guitar *Headstock* functions as a platform upon which the tuning gears (machine heads) are attached. Acoustic, steel-string and electric guitars have a flat head-stock with the capstans mounted through the headstock. The capstan (or "peg") has a hole in which the end of the string is inserted before being "wound-on". Before replacing a string, carefully observe how the strings are wound onto the capstans — there is a right and a wrong way!

NUT. The *Nut* is a white piece of material; synthetic on less expensive instruments, bone or ivory on more expensive guitars. The nut is the termination point of the string — the stopping point of the vibrating string. The nut has grooves cut at pre-set depth, into which the strings sit. The grooves keep the strings separated and determine how high the strings are off the fingerboard. The depth of the grooves set the "action" (or "feel") of the string when playing.

THE FINGERBOARD. The *Fingerboard*, also called "fretboard", is a piece of hard wood glued on top of the neck with grooves in which the frets are placed. The fingerboard may have twelve to twenty-six frets, depending upon the guitar. The Classical instrument has a short neck, the solid body electric has a long neck (more frets). The fingerboard may be flat on classical and flamenco guitars, and curved on most steel-string acoustic and electric guitars.

THE NECK. The *Neck* is a carved piece of wood, usually cut from hardwood such as mahogany, maple or rosewood. The neck may be of one-piece construction, or made of built-up laminated sections. Most guitars will have a *Truss Rod* mounted inside the neck to prevent the neck from warping. A warped neck will make the guitar most difficult to play.

THE BRIDGE. The *Bridge* performs two functions. On the acoustic guitar it supports the saddle, which terminate the vibrating length of the string, and also transmits the strings vibrating energy into the guitar top — the soundboard. On solid-body electric guitars, the bridge and saddle stop the string vibrations. The string's energy is picked up by a magnetic pickup and converted into alternating current. Flat-top acoustic guitars have fixed bridge which are glued onto the top of the soundboard. The strings pass over the saddle and are anchored directly into the bridge with bridge pins.

THE SADDLE. The *Saddle (*made of bone, ivory or plastic) is mounted in a groove cut into the bridge. It may have a rounded or angled top edge. Usually, the saddle will be shaped with the bass string end larger than the treble string end, thereby raising the bass strings higher off the fingerboard. This prevents the heavier vibration of the larger bass strings from "buzzing" the frets. A properly fitting saddle is important. High strings create high string action, making playing much more difficult. Low string action may cause the strings to buzz.

KNOW YOUR GUITAR

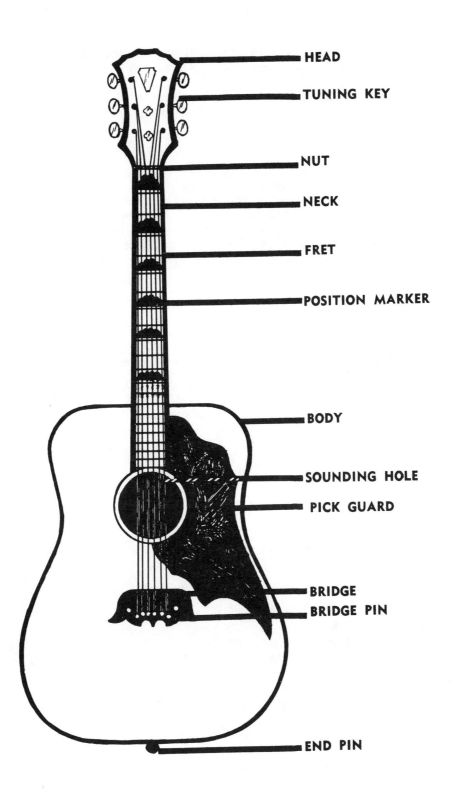

HEAD

TUNING KEY

NUT

NECK

FRET

POSITION MARKER

BODY

SOUNDING HOLE

PICK GUARD

BRIDGE

BRIDGE PIN

END PIN

HOW TO HOLD THE GUITAR

It would seem that any sensible person could sit down with the guitar and hold it in the proper position to strum the strings. However, there is a correct way — one few beginners realize.

The right hand (strumming hand) can comfortably reach the strings from almost any position, even lying down! The right hand is not the problem. It is the left hand (fingering hand) that requires proper positioning.

The guitar must be held close to the body with the right arm balancing the instrument. The left hand should not be required to support the neck.

The guitar should be held almost vertically, in a comfortable position. It will be necessary, at first, to tilt the bottom out slightly so you can see the fingerboard. Do not let it lay flat. The further you lay the guitar over, the harder it is to place the fingers around the neck. Keep the head of the guitar high. Do not point it at the floor.

The right arm should be over the large bout of the guitar, balancing the instrument on your lap (in a sitting position). The right arm should be placed to allow the right hand to comfortably strum the strings over the sound hole (acoustic guitars). Keep the wrist straight with the forearm. By rotating the wrist or using a slight up-down motion of the forearm, you can easily strum across all six strings.

LEFT HAND/WRIST. The strings must be fretted by the tips of the fingers. Only by developing proper left hand placement can you play chords easily and create clear tones.

The left hand wrist should always be arched, the fingers curved over the fingerboard, and placed just behind the frets. The thumb should be planted at the center of the neck, placed under the first finger. Improper placement of the palm and thumb is a common fault of all beginners. Use the thumb for support and *keep* the palm away from the neck. If the guitar is sitting properly, you should not need to hold the neck up. When the palm is against the neck, it becomes difficult to finger the strings properly. When pressing a string down, place the finger behind the fret, not on it, or too far behind it. Take your time and learn each thing well. Remember, the things that seem hard and often impossible today will be easy tomorrow. Don't become discouraged.

HOW THE LEFT HAND FINGERS ARE NUMBERED. Unlike playing the piano, the thumb of the left hand is not normally used to play the guitar and is not counted as a finger. The first finger is the *Number One* finger — the little finger is *Number Four*.

FINGER NAILS. To play the guitar, we use the ends of our fingers. You *must* keep your fingernails clipped short.

CALLOUSES. It is very difficult for beginning students to press the strings down and obtain a clear sound while the string is plucked. This problem is caused by two things: Poor guitar necks, where the strings are abnormally high; and soft fingers. Press a string down and observe the end of your finger. The string leaves a depression. Callouses will prevent this and will make fingering easier. You will have sore fingers, at first. However, callouses will develop quickly, if you keep practicing.

STRUMMING THE GUITAR

Sounds are created on the guitar by striking the strings, causing them to vibrate. There are several ways this may be accomplished. Many guitarists use only their fingers. Some use fingers and a thumb pick. However, the most commonly used method is the *Flat Pick*. We recommend the pick, and pictures in this book show the proper usage of the "pick". The pick should slide down across the strings in a pulling motion. Observe the angle of the pick in relation to the strings in the picture on the following page. Gently strum the strings. You do *not* want a hard stroke. You do not have to beat the strings to make a pleasant sound. Hold the pick loosely, and use a gentle stroking action. Playing loud does not make you play better.

STRUMMING THE GUITAR

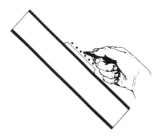

HOLDING THE GUITAR

PICK ANGLE

KEEP THE PALM AWAY FROM NECK

FRETTING STRING PROPERLY

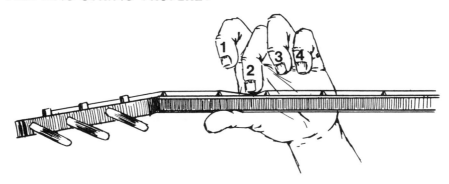

KEEP FINGERS OVER TOP OF NECK

Each string of the guitar must be tuned to a specific pitch. Unless you have been born with the ability to hear perfect pitch, it will be necessary to purchase either a tuning fork, pitch pipe or an electronic meter. The guitar may be tuned to a piano. However, the first-time player would initially be well-advised to seek yet another time-proven method ... let an experienced player tune the instrument. Your local music store will also gladly help you. The ability to tune the guitar properly requires *ear training* (learning to recognize the individual tone of each string).

It is important to have a starting place, a reference or known pitch to which we can tune. A tuning device establishes the starting point. However, if you must tune without a known pitch, lower the string tension on all six strings until they are loose (like rubber bands). Then, bring the tension up on the 6th string until it frets properly (does not rattle on the frets). With practice, you will be very close to proper pitch. We can now use the tone produced on the 6th string, fifth fret, as a reference point to tune the open 5th string.

Pluck the fretted 6th string (fifth fret — note *A*) and tune the open 5th string (the *A* string) to the pitch of the 6th string fretted note — a process called tuning *In Unison*. Continue this process and tune each of the remaining strings. Five strings are tuned at the fifth fret. The third string is an exception; it is tuned at the fourth fret.

HOW THE STRINGS ARE NUMBERED

6TH. The large wound string is the sixth string. Tuned properly, it produces an *E* note, two octaves below middle *C* on the piano.

5TH. The next string down is the fifth string, and properly tuned, is an *A* note.

4TH. The next string is the fourth string, the *D* string.

3RD. The next string is the third string, the *G* string. The *G* string may be plain or wound depending upon the player's string preference.

2ND. Next is the second string, the *B* string.

1ST. The smallest string is the first string (the *High E* string), *E* above middle *C* on the piano.

TUNING FORK *(Illustration Two)*. The tuning fork enables us to tune one string to concert pitch, then tune the other strings as previously explained. The standard tuning fork is pitched to *A*/440 Hz, and is called *Concert Pitch*. This note is equal to the note *A*, 1st string, fifth fret. The open 5th string (*A*), is two octaves lower.

PITCH PIPE *(Illustration Three)*. The pitch pipe is a vibrating reed instrument and produces a relative tone for each string of the guitar. Pitch pipes are not always accurate, the reeds become dirty, and can only be used to tune the guitar to relative pitch.

TUNING METER *(Illustration Four)*. The tuning meter has become very popular and offers a *visual* method of tuning the guitar to concert pitch. On a typical meter, an electronic signal, lights or meter hand will indicate the proper vibrating pitch of the string when accurately tuned.

PIANO *(Illustration Five)*. The guitar may be tuned directly from a piano keyboard. Locate middle *C* on the keyboard, then sound the *E* note above middle *C* and tune the first string (*E*) in unison. Each string may be tuned as shown. The 6th string (*E*) will be two octaves below the first string (*E*).

NOTE: When each string is brought up to pitch, additional stress is placed on the instrument. The strings stretch, the neck bends, and the top flexes, causing the tone of each string to droop slightly in pitch. When you have tuned all six strings, you will find all strings will be slightly below pitch, requiring you to go back and make minor adjustments — fine tuning each string.

You must be able to recognize immediately if a string is too high or too low, so that you can adjust it accordingly. When tuning without a "tuning device", and relying upon your ear, always start by setting the pitch of the 6th string and tune all other strings from this starting pitch. Should you try to set the starting pitch on the 1st string, also an *E* note, you will most probably tune too high, resulting in broken strings and a damaged instrument. Should you become confused, always let the string tension down, and *then* come up in pitch.

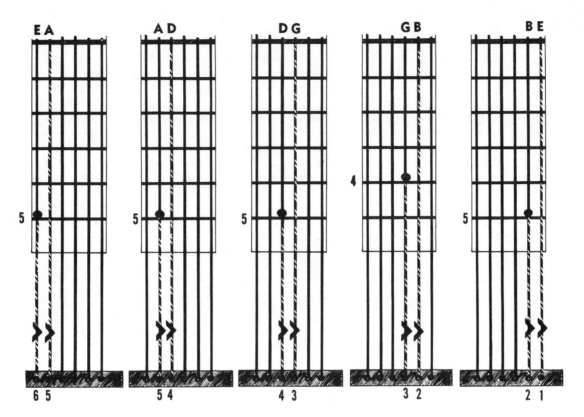

ILLUSTRATION FIVE

THE PIANO KEYBOARD

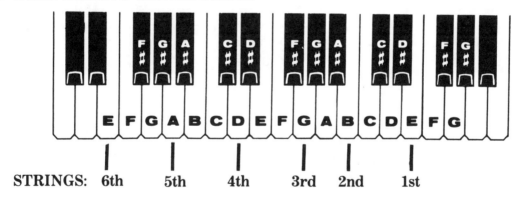

ILLUSTRATION TWO   ILLUSTRATION THREE   ILLUSTRATION FOUR

TUNING FORK

PITCH PIPE

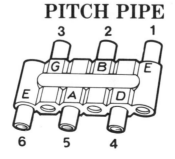

METER

Study a written arrangement and you will most likely find the song's rhythm is built upon three chords. This three-chord progression is used in virtually every song. The three-chord progression represents the building blocks of all musical composition.

Strum a random series of chords, and you will quickly realize not all chords work well together. It will be obvious that some sound better together than others. How do we know which combination of chords will work properly?

We can identify these chords by using a simple rule of music theory. Most of our contemporary music of today can be harmonized with chords built upon the first, fourth and fifth notes of the scale (key) in which the song is written or played.

There are several terms that may be applied to these three chords. The first chord is the *Tonic*, or first chord, build upon the first note of the scale. The second chord is the *Sub-Dominant*, built upon the fourth note of the scale. The third chord of the three-chord progression is built upon the *Dominant*, or fifth note of the scale. These chords may also be identified by Roman Numerals: I IV V *(Illustrations One and Four)*.

Why are these three chords so important and why do they always sound good together regardless of the key played? Between these three chords, every note of the eight-note scale of which music is written, has been used; and individual notes appear in more than one chord.

Illustration Two represents a chord (three or more tones) as seen on an oscilloscope. A melody *(Illustration Three)* is a series of tones rising and falling in pitch with a large degree of variation between the higher and lower tones. It is not possible to use only one chord for playing rhythm. A chord must harmonize with the melody notes. This is to say that each melody note must be a note of a chord or a note very close in the scale, called a passing tone. When the melody no longer harmonizes with the chord, we must change chords.

SIMPLE CHORD CONSTRUCTION

A melody is a series of single notes played in succession. Two notes sounded together create harmony. Three or more notes sounded simultaneously create a chord. A minimum of three notes form a chord on any instrument. In fact, the proper three notes played singularly on three different instruments would produce a chord!

On the guitar, it is possible to play chords with as many as six different notes. However, most six-string chords are comprised of duplicated notes. Simple three-note chords are called *Triads*.

Chords convey two important musical statements. The chord receives its name from the note of the scale upon which the chord is constructed, called the *Root Note*, and is the principle note of the chord. The other two notes add "harmony", creating the sound of the chord.

Chords may be altered (made into a *Minor*, *Diminished* or *Augmented*), and may be extended by adding additional notes of the scale from which the first note is taken (6th, 7th, 9th, 11th and 13th chords). These extended chords are four-note chords extended across all six strings.

The best way to understand how three-chord progression theory works is to familiarize yourself with the sounds created by these chords. Music is a continuous up and down movement of tones, moving above the range of the tonic chord or below it. Sometimes the movement is smooth. Other times, abrupt; and it may skip in small or large intervals (distance between notes). How can you determine which chord should be used, when to change chords, and what should be the next chord played?

The Tonic (I) chord sets the pitch, it is the Key chord — the starting point. In the key of *C*, the tonic chord is *C*. The Sub-Dominant (IV) chord *F*, will sound higher in pitch. The Dominant (V) chord *G7*, will sound lower. Chords are either static, or create tonal movement. The Tonic chord is at rest, static, you can strum it once or a hundred times and your ear will be satisfied. The Sub-Dominant chord, in the three-chord progression, will sound higher in pitch than the Tonic chord. It creates movement and will eventually move either to the Dominant chord, or back to the Tonic. The Dominant chord creates a very unstable movement and demands resolution back to the Tonic.

The Tonic chord is much like standing with both feet on the ground — comfortable, at rest. The tonal movement of the Sub-Dominant chord is much like stopping on one foot — ok, but you will want to move on or come to a complete rest. Stopping on the Dominant chord is like trying to stand on your big toe! You may pause momentarily, however you must either put both feet on the ground or fall.

As you practice playing chords, learn them by key groups, that is the way chords are used. Train your ear to hear how each chord sounds, be aware of the chord's tonal movement. Ear training is as important as memorizing chord fingerings.

A chord may be three strings or four strings, depending upon usage. The tonal character of a chord is derived from the notes played on the high strings (the 1st, 2nd and 3rd strings). Adding notes on the lower strings (the 4th, 5th and 6th strings), impart a fuller sound and add more "power" to rhythm playing.

THE DOMINANT 7th CHORD

C7, G7, E7, B7 and *F7* are examples of Dominant 7th chords. Why do we have Dominant 7th chords? The Dominant chord creates an unsettled tonal movement and usually resolves (moves) to the Tonic chord. The addition of the lowered seventh note of the scale to the basic three-note triad creates an even more unstable sound, one the ear tells us must be resolved. Adding this one additional note to the Dominant chord gives the three-chord progression a definite sense of movement. Train your ear to hear the Dominant 7th chord. It tells you the next chord change will be back to the Tonic chord.

ILLUSTRATION ONE

THE C MAJOR DIATONIC SCALE

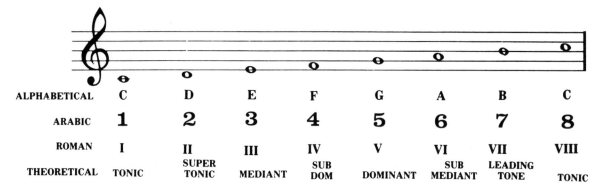

ALPHABETICAL	C	D	E	F	G	A	B	C
ARABIC	1	2	3	4	5	6	7	8
ROMAN	I	II	III	IV	V	VI	VII	VIII
THEORETICAL	TONIC	SUPER TONIC	MEDIANT	SUB DOM	DOMINANT	SUB MEDIANT	LEADING TONE	TONIC

ILLUSTRATION TWO

CHORD: SIX TONES
(GUITAR)

ILLUSTRATION THREE

MELODY: ONE NOTE

ILLUSTRATION FOUR

MELODY AND CHORDS

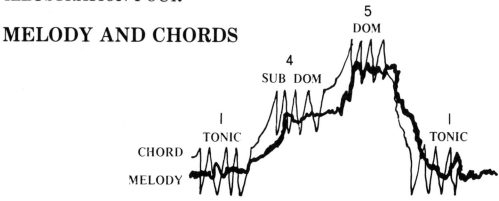

ILLUSTRATION FIVE

DOMINANT CHORD
Lowered One Octave

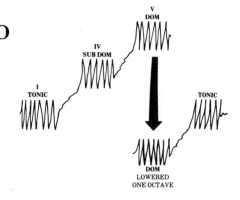

HOW TO READ CHORD DIAGRAMS

The chord diagrams used in this book have been developed to show you where to place your fingers to play each chord. The numbers indicate the proper finger to use on each string and fret. The numbers for the fingers have been placed in the most practical and complete position for each chord. While there are several different fingerings possible for most of these chords, learn to play them as presented.

The illustration shows the proper fingering for the A chord. At all times, keep the fingers directly behind the frets (as indicated in the diagrams). Press firmly to assure all strings will sound properly. If a string buzzes, check the fingering and press harder. Be sure the fingernails are clipped short. To properly fret the strings, you must use the ends of the fingers. Until you have developed callouses, you will find the strings difficult to fret regardless of what you do. Eliminating this problem requires steady, daily practice. Eventually, the skin on the pads of the fingers will harden. Then, you will find it requires less pressure to fret the string.

When a chord diagram indicates that one finger should fret two strings and you are unable to do so, it is permissible to leave off the lowest sounding tone. If the unfretted string is going to be struck with the pick when strumming, it should be muted or deadened with the other fingers.

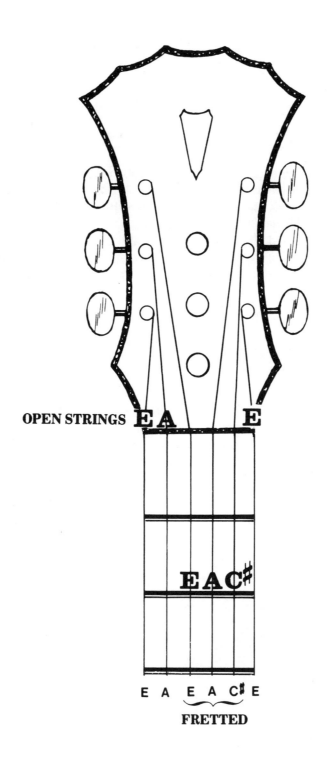

OPEN STRINGS **E A** **E**

E A C#

E A   E A C# E

FRETTED

OPEN CHORDS/CLOSED CHORDS

There are two types of chords: "Open string" chords and "closed" chords. The closed chord does not utilize any open, unfretted strings. In a closed chord, each string played must be fretted. Closed chords, commonly called Barre Chords, may be "half-barre" or "full-barre", depending on how many strings are played. Closed chords place a great deal of stress on the left hand. A full-barre chord requires the first finger to be extended across all six strings. It requires a tremendous amount of hand strength to successfully play barre chords and is beyond the ability of most beginners.

Open string chords may be as simple as using one finger and at the most, requires three fingers. Open string chords are a combination of fretted notes and those tones produced by the open unfretted strings. Eventually, as you progress as a guitarist, you will need to learn both forms.

Open string chords are thought of as "beginner chords". However, all guitarists use open string chords, even Rock players. The open, unfretted strings produce an after-ring. They continue to vibrate even if the hand is removed from the fingerboard. Open string chords also create the lowest tones and work well in the keys of: *E*, *A*, *D*, *G* and *C* major. These keys are used extensively by Folk, Country and Blue Grass musicians.

The chords presented in this book are open string chords and are presented in the Three-Chord Progression group, since that is how chords are used to create music.

OPEN STRING
G CHORD

CLOSED (BARRED)
F CHORD

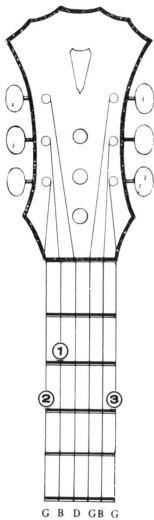

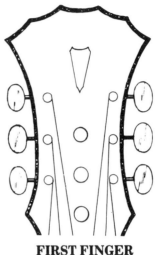

FIRST FINGER BARRED

ROOT NOTE

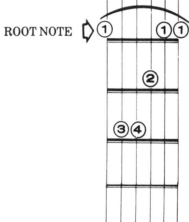

G B D GB G

F C F A C F

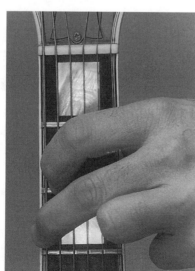

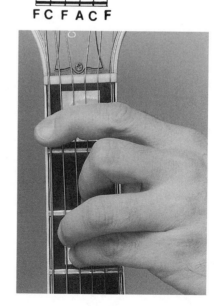

TONIC

C
CEG

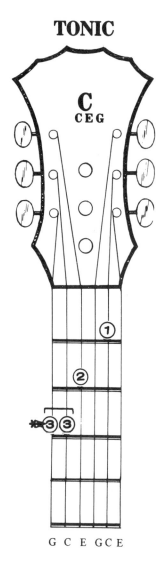

G C E G C E

SUB DOM

F
FAC

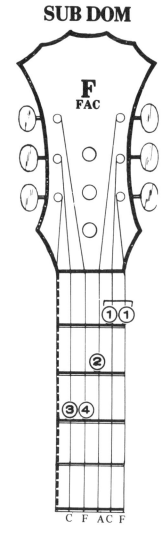

C F AC F

DOM 7

G7
GBDF

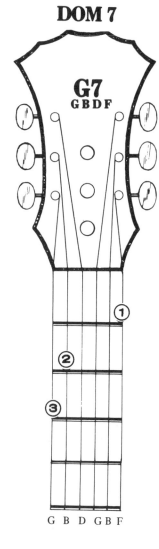

G B D GB F

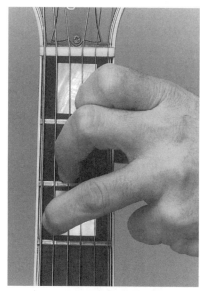

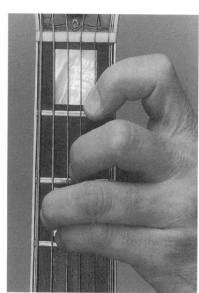

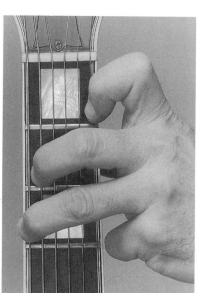

TONIC

D
D F# A

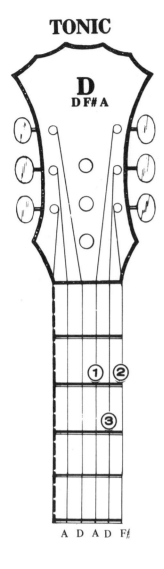

A D A D F#

SUB DOM

G
G B D

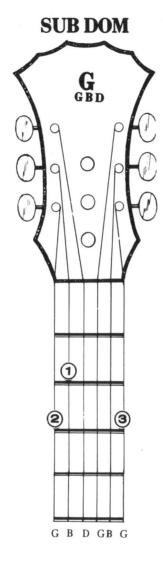

G B D GB G

DOM 7

A7
A C# E G

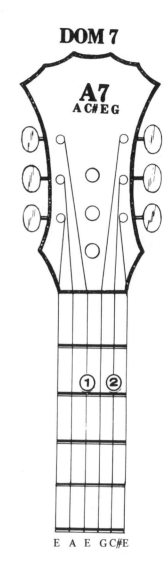

E A E G C#E

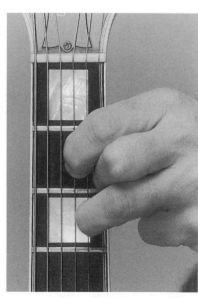

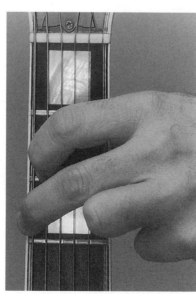

TONIC

E
E G# B

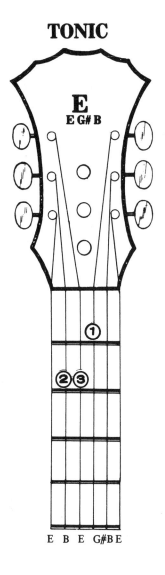

E B E G#B E

SUB DOM

A
A C# E

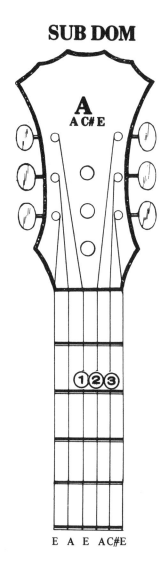

E A E AC#E

DOM 7

B7
B D# F# A

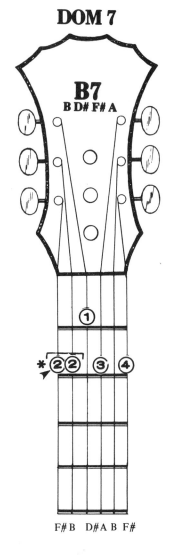

F# B D#A B F#

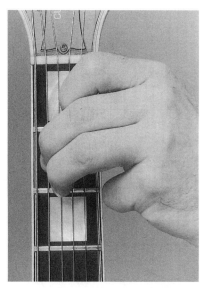

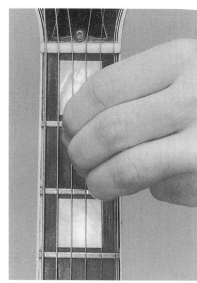

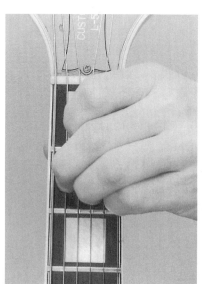

TONIC

F
FAC

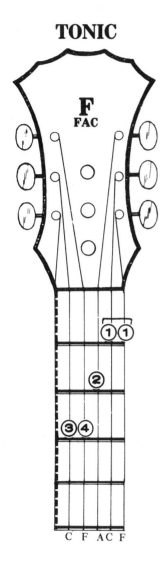

C F AC F

SUB DOM

B♭
B♭ D F

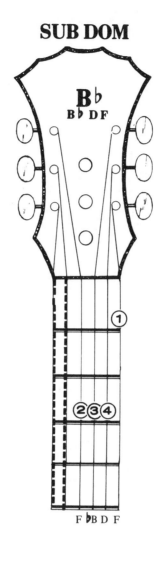

F ♭B D F

DOM 7

C7
C E G B♭

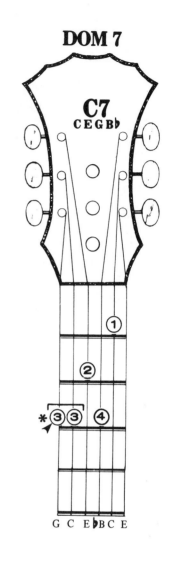

G C E ♭B C E

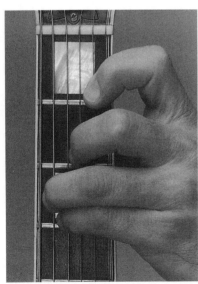

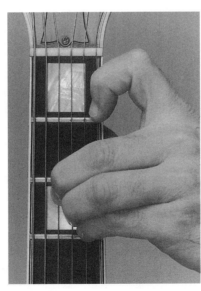

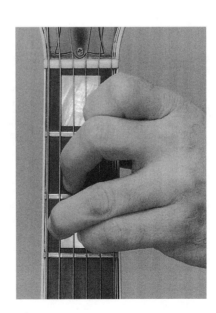

TONIC

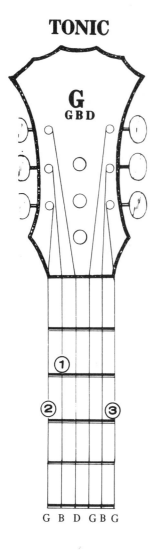

G B D G B G

SUB DOM

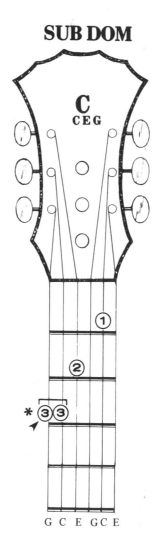

G C E G C E

DOM 7

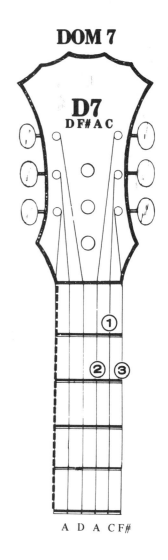

A D A C F#

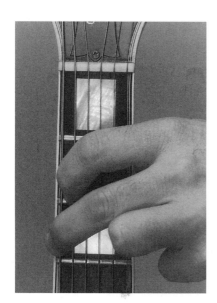

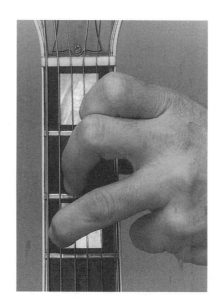

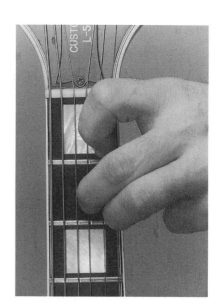

*Optional Fingering   Do not play strings indicated by dotted liens.

TONIC

A
A C# E

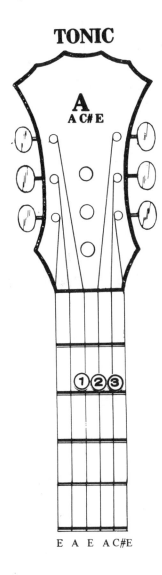

E A E A C# E

SUB DOM

D
D F# A

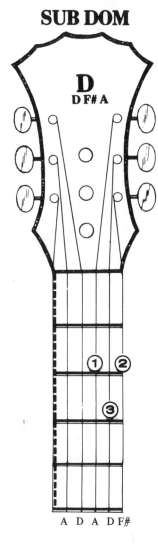

A D A D F#

DOM 7

E7
E B G# D

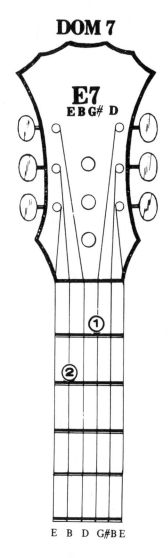

E B D G# B E

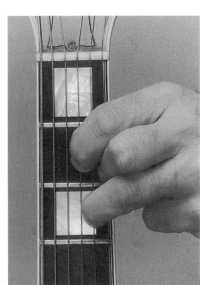

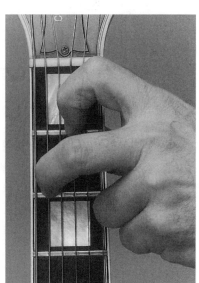

*Do not play strings indicated by dotted lines.

ALPHABETICAL LISTING

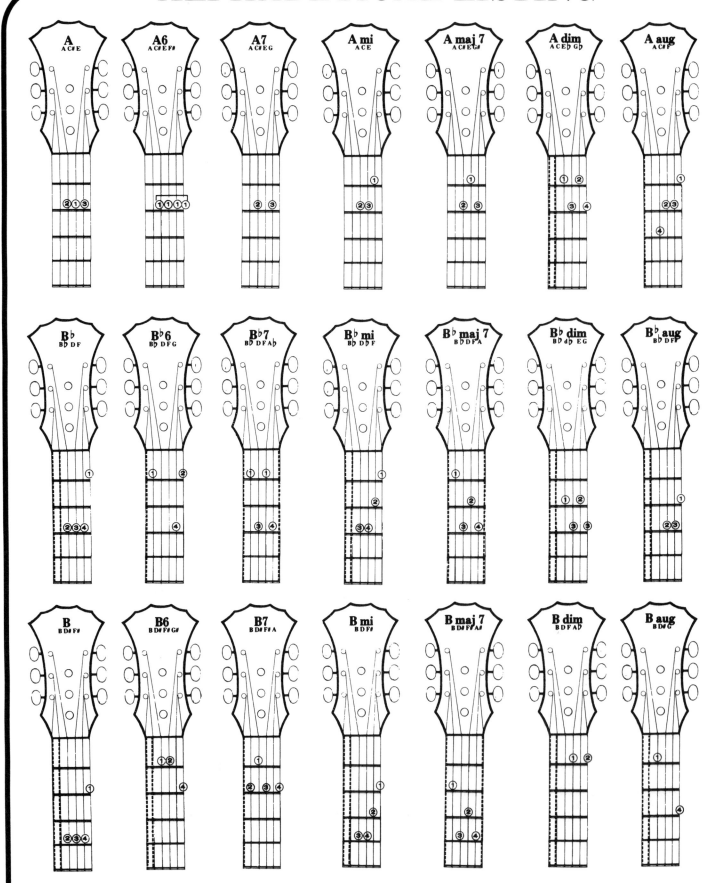

*Optional Fingering

*Do not play strings indicated by dotted lines.

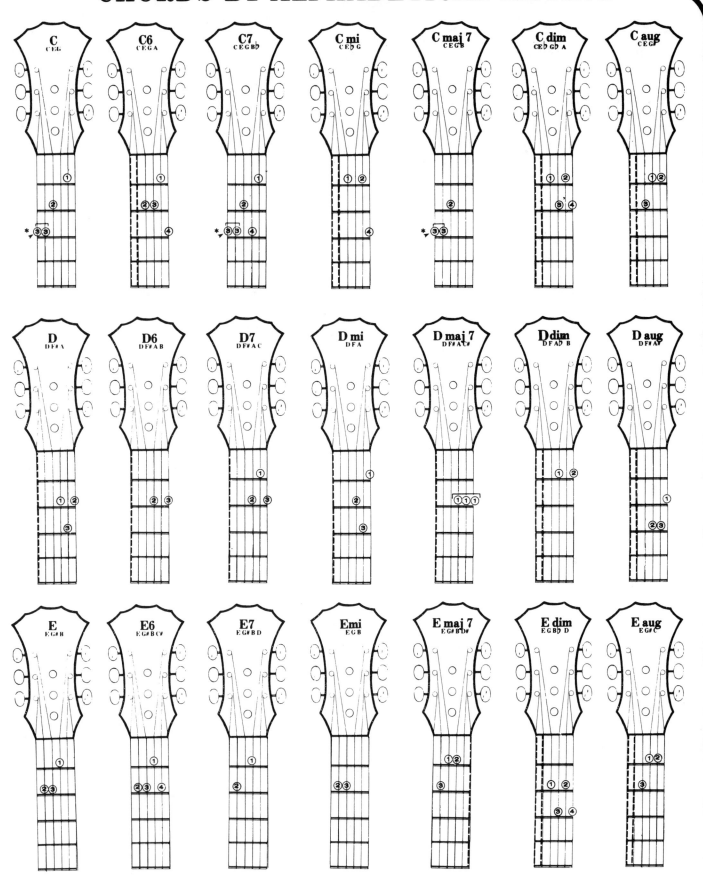

*Optional Fingering   *Do not play strings indicated by dotted lines.

THE ART OF STRUMMING RHYTHM

THE ART OF PLAYING RHYTHM

All music composition is a combination of *Time, Harmony* and *Melody;* and are of course, interdependent.

Time is the *Horizontal* effect of music. Time moves on two planes: *Tempo,* how fast the arrangement is played expressed in beats per minute; *Time Signature,* how many beats per measure. Timing also involves the ability to play evenly, maintaining a constant beat — an even rhythm, and to play notes at precisely the same time as other musicians in the band.

Harmony represents the *Vertical* principle of music. Harmony is created by "stacking" notes. Chords are three or more note stacked one above the other and sounded at one time.

Melody is the study and usage of scales. Melody is the horizontal movement of single tones, fluctuating up and down within the spectrum of the scale to create a recognizable tune.

Rhythm guitar playing creates beat, tempo and harmony. Rhythm sets the "feel" of the piece being played — establishes the identity of the song. Good rhythm players not only have developed a vast repertoire of chords, they have the ability to "hear" chord changes, and can anticipate the next chord in the chord progression. They have developed the ability to play a song, from beginning to end, without changing speed.

Timing (to play even tempo) can be difficult, especially for the new player who is also struggling with unfamiliar fingering positions. However, learning to play in proper time is a basic discipline, one that can be cultivated.

SIMPLE TIME SIGNATURES
(Illustration One)

The *Time Signature* tells the rhythm guitarists how many beats there are within each measure, how many taps of your foot. The simplest and most often used time signature is 4/4. This is called *Four-Four* time, and is often abbreviated to "C", meaning *Common Time*. In this time signature, there are four beats within each measure, four down beats. The 3/4 time signature means three beats to each measure and is called *Waltz Time*. The 2/4 time signature means two beats to each measure.

COUNTING TIME/KEEPING BEAT
(Illustration Two)

Music is the science of *Timing* and *Rhythm*. You cannot play the guitar alone or in a group if you do not develop a keen sense of these two important aspects of music. You have seen musicians keeping time by tapping their foot. This is a way of counting time and enables them to maintain an even beat.

The *Counting Time Diagram* shows the proper technique of the foot tapping the floor on the *Down Beat*. Tap your foot on the count: *One, Two, Three, Four*, etc., the down beat. On every count, your foot taps the floor. Tap at any speed (tempo) you desire, however you must keep the beat even. Maintain a constant beat.

THE STAFF — TIME SIGNATURES

ILLUSTRATION ONE

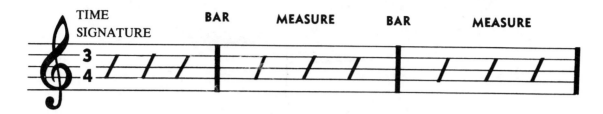

3/4 TIME

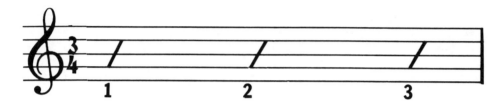

4/4 TIME

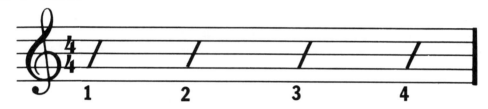

ILLUSTRATION TWO

COUNTING TIME

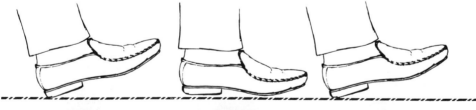

UP BEAT	DOWN BEAT One	UP BEAT
COUNT: AND	. One	. AND
READY	STRUM	READY

READING THE RHYTHM PART OF AN ARRANGEMENT

Music is written on a five-line staff, divided into equal measures. The guitar and vocal part is written on the *Treble Staff (Illustration One)*. Time signatures indicate the number of beats within each measure *(Illustration Two)*. Chord symbols written above the appropriate words within each measure tell the rhythm guitarist where changes occur *(Illustration Three)*. Normally, chord changes take place *on* the beat, and the placement of the chord symbol within the measure will indicate the appropriate beat.

PLAYING INSTRUCTIONS — SYMBOLS

Most music involves a great deal of repetition, and arrangers use special direction symbols to indicate repeat passages *(Illustration Four)*.

REPEAT SIGNS. When you come to a pair of double dots placed to the *left* of a double bar line, go back to the measure where double dots are placed to the *right* of a double bar, and repeat this section (play everything between the double dots). Should you come to a repeat sign and there is not a second indication (double bar with dots to the right), then go back to the beginning and repeat the entire section back to the double dots.

FIRST AND SECOND ENDINGS. An arrangement may have two endings — one, a "turn-around", taking the song back to the beginning, the second continuing through to the end of the piece. The first time through, play the section marked (1), return to the beginning and play through until you come back to the first ending — skip 1 (omitting ending 1), and play the second ending (marked 2).

DA CAPO (D.C.). Da capo, abbreviated to D.C., means from the beginning. When you come upon this sign, go back to the beginning and play the arrangement again.

AL CODA. Al coda (Al ⊕) means "to the end". This symbol tells you to skip to the   (the coda sign), and play through to the end.

DAL SEGUO (D.S.: 𝄋). Dal seguo means "from the beginning". When you come to D.S.: 𝄋, go back in the arrangement to the sign ·𝄋, and repeat from this symbol.

STRUMMING RHYTHM PATTERNS
(pages 30 - 31)

Strumming should be an instinctive action, the *right hand* rotation (movement) should be with the beat — hand and pick moving down across the strings on the down beat, moving upward on the upbeat. The most basic strums are upstrokes and downstrokes. We can also use the "pick-n-strum" style, alternating a plucked bass note with the strumming.

STRUMMING THE BEAT

The beat is comprised of the down beat and the up beat, also called the *Back Beat*. In simplest usage, we strum down each time we tap our foot, this is called *Down Beat* strumming *(Illustration One)*.

Practice down beat strumming — keep the right hand rotation in sync with your foot. In down beat strumming, we are ascending down strums, only lightly brushing the strings on the up beat, if at all. On the down stroke, strum all the strings (if the chord is a six-string chord). On the up stroke, if the strings are brushed, we only play the treble strings (the 1st, 2nd, 3rd and 4th strings). We do not intentionally sound the bass strings.

DOWN/UP STRUMS *(Illustration Two)*. This is an effective strumming technique, creating lots of tonal movement — a busy sound. Rotate the wrist in sync with your foot. Count: 1 down, and ⁻ up stroke (1 and 2 and 3 and 4 and). Keep moving and ascend the down stroke, the down beat.

SYNCOPATION ON THE 2ND BEAT *(Illustration Three)*. This is a more complex rhythm patter. The count: 1 2 and 3 4, placing an upbeat strum between the second and third beat.

PICK-N-STRUM *(Illustration Four)*. The pick-n-strum technique utilizes an alternating bass note with down strums. Normally, we pick the bass string that produces the Root tone of the chord — the note upon which the chord structure is built; G chord, the root note is G, located on the third fret, 6th string. Pick this on the first beat, strum and pick the next higher bass, the fifth string, on the third beat.

BASS NOTE AND SYNCOPATION STRUMS *(Illustration Five)*. Pick the Root note of the chord, then strum using the up-down strum. Count: 1 2 and 3 and 4.

WALTZ STRUMS *(Illustration Six)*. Waltzes are played in 3/4 time, which effectively limits the type of rhythm patterns. You can strum the down beat; one down stroke followed by two down-up strums. The most effective rhythm pattern is pick, strum, strum.

NOTE: Rhythm playing can be a life-long learning endeavor. Just "beating" chords will not make you a good rhythm guitarist. Every new chord position will require hours of practice. Learning new rhythmic patterns, developing the ability to adapt an appropriate pattern to a new song; learning to hear chords and anticipate changes, will not come easily. However, if you take your time and practice, you can become an accomplished guitarist. Remember, whatever you play — play it well. You will be surprised how many great songs utilize simple chords and unsophisticated chord patterns. Become the best you can be. That alone will make you better than most players!

ILLUSTRATION ONE

THE RHYTHM PART OF AN ARRANGEMENT
THE TREBLE CLEF

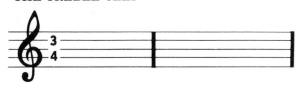

ILLUSTRATION TWO

TIME SIGNATURES

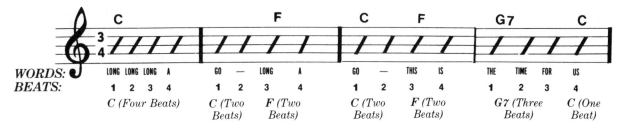

ILLUSTRATION THREE

WHERE CHANGES OCCUR

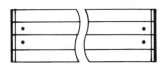

WORDS: LONG LONG LONG A   GO — LONG A   GO — THIS IS   THE TIME FOR US

BEATS: 1 2 3 4   1 2 3 4   1 2 3 4   1 2 3 4

C (Four Beats)   C (Two Beats)   F (Two Beats)   C (Two Beats)   F (Two Beats)   G7 (Three Beats)   C (One Beat)

ILLUSTRATION FOUR

REPEAT SIGNS

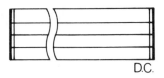

When you come to the second sign, you go back to the first and repeat the section in between the two double bar signs.

FIRST & SECOND ENDINGS.

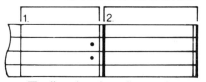

The first time through, you play the section marked 1. Then, go back to the beginning and, on the second time through, play the section marked 2 (omitting section 1).

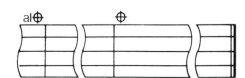

DA CAPO. Often abbreviated to D.C., da capo means "from the head". When you see this sign, you must go back to the beginning of the piece of music.

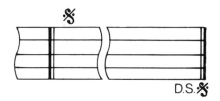

DAL SEGNO. Instead of going right back to the beginning, go back only as far as the sign. Dal segno means "from the sign", and is abbreviated as D.S.

AL CODA. Meaning "to the tail", this tells you that you must go to the end section, which starts with a coda sign.

TYPES OF STRUMS

ILLUSTRATION ONE
DOWN BEAT STRUMS

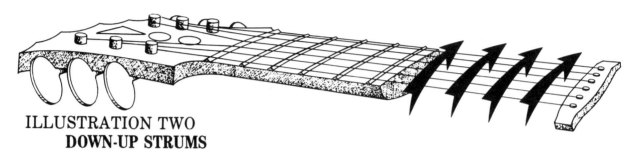

ILLUSTRATION TWO
DOWN-UP STRUMS

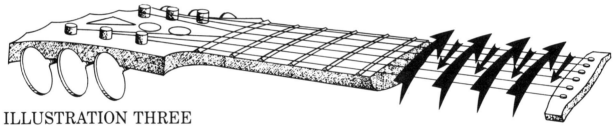

ILLUSTRATION THREE

SYNCOPATION ON SECOND BEAT

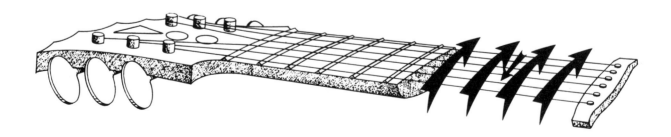

ILLUSTRATION FOUR
PICK-N-STRUM

ILLUSTRATION FIVE
BASS NOTE AND SYNCOPATION

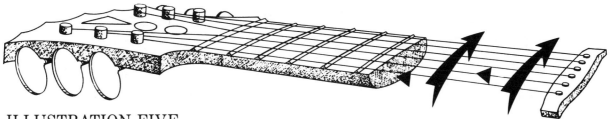

ILLUSTRATION SIX
WALTZ STRUM

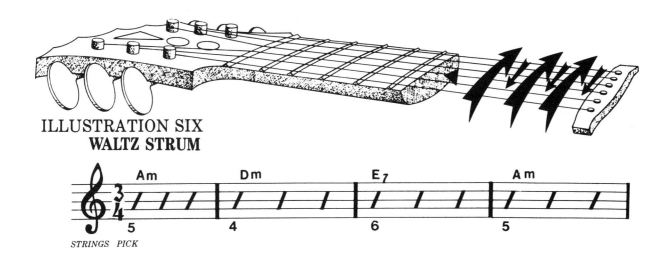

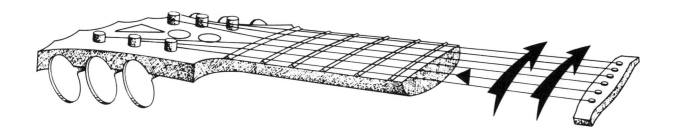